HOW ARE THEY BUILT?

BRIDGES

Lynn M. Stone

Rourke Publishing LLC
Vero Beach, Florida 32964

www.rourkepublishing.com

PHOTO CREDITS:
Cover, pages 4, 10, 18, 32 ©Photo Disc, Inc.; pages 8, 24, 26, 29©Lynn M. Stone; page 7 ©James P. Rowan; page 20 ©Armentrout; pages 21, 23, 25, 30 ©Dynamic Design; page 35 © AP/Wide World; pages 15, 26, 17, 31, 39, 40, 42 ©Finley McNary Engineers, Inc.

EDITORIAL SERVICES:
Pamela Schroeder

ABOUT THE AUTHOR
Lynn Stone is the author of more than 400 children's books. He is a talented natural history photographer as well. Lynn, a former teacher, travels worldwide to photograph wildlife in its natural habitat.

Library of Congress Cataloging-in-Publication Data

Stone, Lynn M.
    Bridges / Lynn M. Stone
       p. cm. — (How are they built?)
    Includes bibliographical references and index.
    Summary: Presents information on how bridges are built, their history and various types, and give specific examples of important bridges in North America.
       ISBN 1-58952-135-8
    1. Bridges—Design and construction—Juvenile literature. [1. Bridges—Design and construction.] I. Title

TG148 .S76 2001   200104167
624'.2'097—dc21

Printed In The USA

TABLE OF CONTENTS

An arch bridge spans a narrow gorge, giving pedestrians safe, easy passage from one side to the other.

BRIDGES

Bridges are structures that help us safely cross rivers, bays, swamps, gorges, railroad tracks, and roads. Bridges give us a safe way of going from one place to the other. Without bridges, travel would be far less safe and take much more time.

There are hundreds of thousands of bridges in the United States and Canada alone. Each bridge serves a special purpose at its location. Every bridge has its own story, not only of how it was built, but why it was built.

Bridges can be difficult and costly to build. They are not often built without a good reason. Each bridge solves the problem of getting from one place to another. For example, ferry boats are one way for people to cross a body of water. But if the traffic becomes too great, a bridge may be the solution. The famous Golden Gate Bridge across San Francisco Bay was built in the 1930s for that reason.

Lights twinkle along the Golden Gate Bridge span between Sausalito and San Francisco, California.

This railroad bridge across a Montana river is basically a beam bridge supported by piers built of interlocking beams.

Because each bridge is in a different location, each bridge is unique. Bridges may be plain or even ugly. Bridges may also be dramatic, graceful, and grand. Some of the oldest bridges show "character" in their **architecture** and look.

Different types of bridges have unique parts. However, all bridges share some features. Almost all bridges are supported by at least two structures set firmly in the ground. These structures are **abutments**. Some bridges have **piers**, structures that rise between the abutments to help support the bridge **deck**. The deck is made of beams, or girders. Short bridges, however, may be supported by only their abutments.

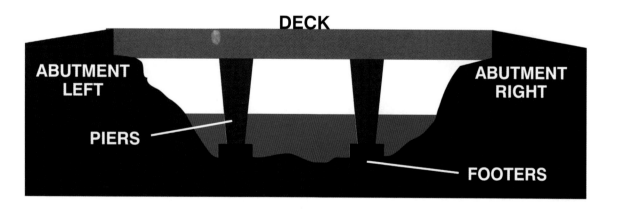

Mighty towers support long steel cables of the famous Brooklyn Bridge in New York.

Suspension bridges have tall structures called **towers**. Towers are built upon the bridge piers. The towers rise well above the level of the bridge deck. The Akashi Kaikyo Bridge in Japan has the tallest bridge towers in the world. They stand 928 feet (283 m). Suspension bridges also have long steel cables that help support the bridge.

A bridge may have one **span** or several. A span is the distance between two bridge supports. The supports may be tall columns, piers, or the rock walls of a gorge. Short bridges tend to be single-span bridges. Longer bridges are multi-span bridges. A multi-span bridge's longest span is the main span.

HISTORY OF BRIDGES

Early humans did not have to look far to discover bridges. The nearest wooded stream bank would have been a good place to look. They would have found fallen trees reaching from one side of the stream to the other. In a short time, people made their own log bridges. Then they made bridges of flat, stone slabs placed upon smaller stepping stones.

The creation of the arched bridge was a major step forward in bridge design. The arch bridge, named for its shape, dates back nearly 5,000 years. The oldest known arch bridge was built in Egypt to cross the Nile River. Arch bridges were later built in ancient China, Greece, Rome, and Babylonia. An arch bridge over the Meles River in Turkey still stands nearly 3,000 years after it was built.

As bridge styles and construction changed, so did bridge building materials. The Romans began using stone instead of wood in their bridges. And in 1779, the first iron bridge was built in Coalbrookdale, England. Less than 100 years later, the first steel bridge was built. That bridge spanned the Mississippi River in St. Louis. Most modern bridges are built of **concrete** reinforced with steel.

WHO BUILDS BRIDGES?

You may have seen bridge construction crews and their heavy equipment—trucks, cranes, and sometimes barges. Construction crews do build bridges, but long before their job begins, other people have already "built" the bridge—on computers!

Architects, along with **engineers**, are the people who design structures. Architects are people with ideas and "vision" about how a bridge or other structure should look. The engineer's job is to determine how to make the architect's idea work. The best looking bridge in the world would be useless if it couldn't support its own weight and that of the cars that cross it. It is the engineer's job to make sure the bridge is safe and solid.

For architects and engineers, designing a bridge means finding answers to some important questions: How great a distance will the bridge span? How high must it be? How much will it cost? What kind of building materials are available? In what kind of soil or rock will the bridge supports be? What natural forces will the bridge face?

Engineers often spend long days on job sites. They must make sure that all of the building plans are followed in detail.

To find answers to these questions, the design team needs help. A **geologist** will study the bedrock at the building site. A **meteorologist** studies the effects of weather on the bridge. Other engineers advise the **client** about which **contractors** might be best to build the bridge.

The client is the person or group of people paying for the bridge to be built. Most bridges are built by governments. Most often it is a part of the government, such as a state department of transportation, that decides whether or not a bridge needs to be built. The government then uses tax dollars to pay for the design and construction of the bridge.

The amount of machinery, materials, and manpower needed to build a single bridge makes it very expensive.

Giant cranes move sections of reinforced concrete during construction of the Sidney Lanier Bridge in Georgia.

The design team has to keep the bridge's cost within the budget. Bridges can be very expensive. Just the main span of the new Sidney Lanier Bridge cost the Georgia Department of Transportation $65 million. But the Akashi Kaikyo Bridge, the world's longest suspension bridge—12,828 feet (3,910 m) long—cost $4.3 billion!

*Most covered bridges are basic beam bridges with
a protective housing of wood.*

18

KINDS OF BRIDGES

Bridge designers decide what kind of bridge will be best for the location. There are several different kinds of bridges, but they fall into three main groups: beam or girder bridges, suspension bridges, and arch bridges.

The very modern and popular **cable-stayed** bridge is a form of suspension bridge. The **truss** bridge is a form of the beam bridge. And the **cantilever** bridge is a form of truss bridge.

The biggest difference in bridges is the distance they can cross in a single span. A modern beam bridge, for example, spans about 200 feet (61m). A modern arch bridge may have an 800 to 1,000-foot (244 to 305-m) span. A suspension bridge can span more than 1 mile (1,609 m).

This modern beam bridge was built to allow boat traffic to pass on the river below.

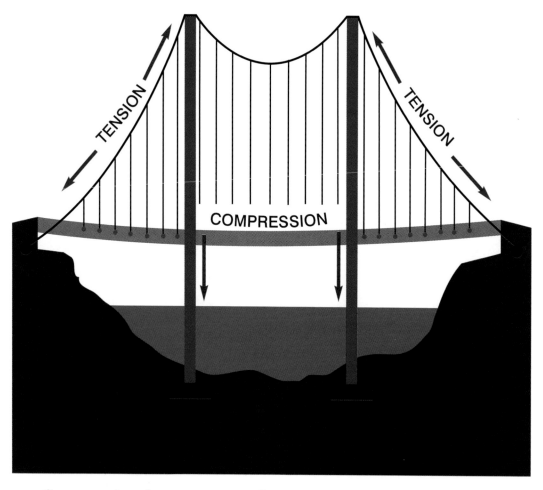

Compression forces try to push a suspension bridge deck down.
The weight of the bridge deck creates tension, stretching the bridge
cables that hold, or suspend, it. This illustration shows how the
deck wants to compress and bring tension in the cables.

Each major type of bridge works in its own way. Each deals differently with two natural forces—**compression** and **tension**. A bridge must handle compression and tension without breaking.

Compression is a force that acts to compress, or shorten. If you sit on a coiled spring, for example, the spring shortens as your weight compresses it. Tension, on the other hand, lengthens. If you grab both ends of the spring and pull, the spring begins to lengthen.

A well-designed bridge solves problems caused by compression and tension. One way it does that is by spreading, or **dissipating**, these forces over a greater area. That way no single, small area of the bridge has to handle all the force. A bridge may also be constructed in such a way as to transfer the force to a stronger area of the bridge.

An arch bridge has an arched, or semi-circular, structure under its deck and abutments on each end. The arch shape spreads the weight from the deck to the abutments. Modern building materials, such as steel and concrete, have made it possible to build longer arch bridges. The New River Gorge Bridge in West Virginia spans 1,700 feet (518 m)!

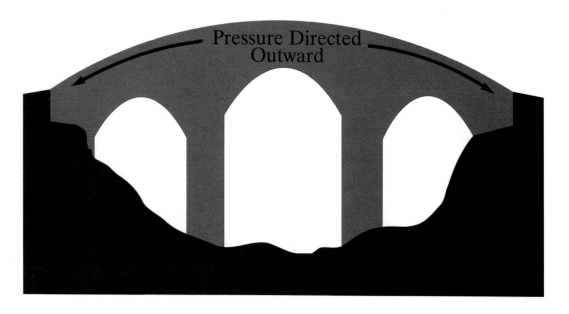

The arch bridge spreads its weight outward putting a great deal of pressure on the abutments.

A pedestrian arch bridge spans a canal in Venice, Italy. The arch allows small boats to slip easily underneath the bridge.

The beam bridge looks almost bench-like. Its deck is built on rigid horizontal beams, or girders, which rest on piers at each end. The weight of the bridge and its traffic pushes down on the piers, which absorb the compression. Beam bridges are the most basic of bridges. They are also less expensive to build and maintain.

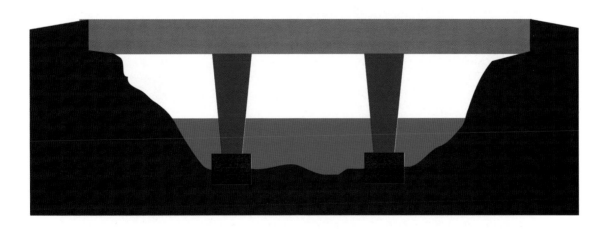

Beam bridges are the least attractive, but the most common, of bridge styles.

Florida's Overseas Highway bridge restricts boat traffic because of the high number of piers beneath its deck.

Most beam bridges are made of pre-stressed concrete—concrete reinforced with steel. But the further apart the beam bridge's supports are, the weaker it is. Beam bridges can cross great distances only if they are linked together. In fact, the world's longest bridge is a beam bridge—the Lake Ponchartrain Causeway in Louisiana. It has two **parallel** two-lane sections. The southbound lane has 2,243 spans. The newer northbound lane has 1,500 spans. The bridge stretches nearly 24 miles (39 km)! The problem with this bridge is the large number of piers underneath its deck. They block the passage of large boats. There is a similar problem with Florida's Overseas Highway bridge in the Florida Keys.

In recent years, bridge designers have made stronger beam bridges with the use of I-shaped beams. They are stronger than older beams because they have more material on each edge.

Long ago, bridge designers learned that beams would be stronger if they were supported by trusses. Trusses are frames built in triangular shapes. Some trusses are constructed along the tops of bridge decks. Others are built below the decks. A truss helps the bridge dissipate compression.

Suspension bridges are at the peak of the bridge builder's art. Suspension bridges and their cable-stayed cousins can be used to span great rivers and bays. At the same time, they leave huge open areas underneath for shipping traffic.

This truss bridge in Haddam, Connecticut, is of the swing type. The main span (left) swings away to allow the passage of ships.

When the Golden Gate Bridge was built in the 1930s, the U.S. Navy wanted to make sure that its ships could still sail through the channel underneath the bridge. The bridge's suspension design ensured that the Navy would have its wish.

A large, modern suspension bridge has giant cables from which the bridge deck is attached, or suspended. The cables are stretched across the bridge towers. The cables transfer the compression to the bridge towers. The towers are firmly anchored in the ground, where they dissipate the compression.

A suspension bridge is easily identified by the huge, rope-like steel cables that support its deck.

*Cable stays attach a cable-stayed bridge's deck to
towers that bear the bridge's weight.*

The tension forces on a suspension bridge are
handled by the cables and their **anchorages**. The weight
of the bridge and its traffic stretch the cables. The cable
anchorages are under tension, too. However, the
anchorages are solidly locked into the ground, like the
towers. The tension in the anchorages is dissipated into
the earth or rock.

In a cable-stayed bridge, the cables are attached to
the towers. The towers bear the load rather than
dividing it with the anchorages.

Designers built an arch bridge across this canyon but had to include an unusual curved roadway to accommodate the landscape.

BRIDGES AND NATURE

Bridge designers must take several natural forces into account when they are making plans. Bridge designers have to understand how wind, heat, cold, ice, rain, salt, earthquakes, and vibrations will affect the bridge.

Bridges built along coastlines or on hillsides must allow for natural water runoff or rockslides.

Suspension bridges are more likely to be affected by high winds because they are suspended from cables. Since designers cannot stop the wind, they plan bridges that can control the effects of wind. They may use wind tunnel tests, for example, to test a bridge's design.

When it's hot, a bridge's beams and roadway will expand. Designers build expansion and roller joints into the bridge. That prevents the movement of the expanding bridge from affecting the cars and trucks on the bridge.

Vibrations sometimes can create dangerous shock waves. Powerful vibrations caused by 42-mile (69-km) per hour winds brought down the first Tacoma Narrows Bridge in Washington in 1940. No one died because traffic was stopped before the bridge tore itself apart.

Steady vibrations caused by only moderately strong winds caused the Tacoma Narrows Bridge to shake violently and finally collapse.

Nicknamed "Galloping Gertie," the long, narrow bridge was too flexible. In the four months of its existence, drivers on the bridge complained of motion sickness. Some people drove the bridge just to feel its roller coaster effects! It is from such failures, however, that engineers have learned how to build better, safer bridges.

Japanese engineers faced major problems with nature when they planned the great Akashi Kaikyo Bridge. It was finally completed in 1998. The bridge was built in an area of gale winds, earthquakes, and tidal waves. First, engineers supported the bridge with a truss beneath the roadway. The network of truss triangles makes the bridge rigid, but allows wind to blow through. They also placed 20 wind-dampening units in each tower. When wind sways the bridge, the dampening units swing in the opposite direction. Their motion balances the bridge motion and lessens the sway. This bridge can stand up to 180-mile (292-km) per hour winds and major earthquakes.

BUILDING A BRIDGE

Each bridge has its own design and construction history. No two are alike, but all are interesting. A good example is the cable-stayed Sidney Lanier Bridge in Brunswick, Georgia. The Lanier Bridge, to be completed in 2002, spans the tide-driven Brunswick River.

One of the first projects in the bridge's construction involved drilling shafts into the earth and rock under the river. The shafts for the bridge's two towers were drilled 115 feet (35 m) below sea level. Forty shafts, each 6 feet (2 m) wide, were drilled for each of the two bridge towers. Once dug, the shafts were filled with concrete and **rebar**, which is a framework of steel bars. After the shafts were poured, the bridge builders built a **cofferdam** at each of the two tower sites. Cofferdams are big, boxlike structures. They are set into water, then pumped dry. In the dry environment of the cofferdams, workers could begin work on the concrete structures that would rise above the level of the river bed.

The first structures were footings. Footings are the bridge's "feet." The footings are made of concrete poured over the tops of the deep shafts. The footings are the bases for the columns that make up the bridge's towers. The footings for the two towers are 19 feet (6 m) deep. They were formed after three days of non-stop pouring of concrete.

*Cranes work on the construction of one of the
Sidney Lanier Bridge's towers.*

By pouring liquid concrete onto these steel rods and wire mesh, construction crews will be making reinforced concrete, an extremely strong material.

After the footings were poured, workers could remove the cofferdams. Then they built "islands" of sand and stone around the footings. The islands took 2,400 truckloads of sand and 15,700 truckloads of rock! The islands are designed to protect the bridge supports from being hit by a ship.

With footings in place, construction began on the columns. Bridge piers are usually made of one column. The Lanier Bridge has some two-column piers that are known as **bents**. Another beam, called a cap, reaches across the two columns to form a support frame.

Columns and beams are made of concrete and steel. Some sections are boxlike and hollow. Some sections were made away from the bridge site and shipped in by barge. Other concrete sections, like those for the bridge deck, were poured at the bridge site.

Moving beams—some of which weigh 116 tons (104,504 kg) and are 180 feet (55 m) long—is a tough and dangerous job. There are cranes designed to lift bridge beams. Some of them work from barges and others work from dry land.

Construction of the Lanier Bridge framework began near the shoreline. These parts of bridges are known as the "approaches" because they approach the higher part of the bridge where the towers and main span are.

With cranes lifting and placing beams, the bridge towers were raised to their full height. Meanwhile, with the deck beams placed, workers could begin work on the deck itself. They put the rebar in place and poured the concrete. Trucks equipped with long-armed pumps sent concrete up to the deck on the approaches. For pouring higher spans, concrete trucks drove onto the completed part of the deck, and pumped concrete from there.

Building the deck required the use of **form travelers**. Forms are molds used to shape concrete. Form travelers are just that—traveling forms. With their loads of fresh concrete, they are designed to move into places that are difficult to reach. Piece by piece, the bridge deck grew outward from each tower until finally the main span closed.

Sections of this bridge deck draw closer and closer to meeting.

The Lanier Bridge also needed cable stays. The cable stays were built as needed to brace each new section of deck. Each cable stay is made of steel strands surrounded by a layer of cement grout, a plastic pipe, and white wrapping tape. The grout helps protect the steel from rust. The cables were lifted into place by cranes. The top of each cable was anchored in one of the two towers. The bottom of each was attached to an anchorage inside the deck. Jacks were used to tighten the cables and increase or decrease the tension on them as needed.

The Lanier Bridge plans were formed in 1993. Construction began in July, 1995. Like most big bridge projects, the entire job will take nearly 10 years from start to completion.

IMPORTANT BRIDGES OF NORTH AMERICA

Brooklyn Bridge, New York. Completed in 1883, the Brooklyn Bridge was the first suspension bridge to use steel for its cable wire. It took 14 years to build the 3,460-foot (1,055-m) bridge, which is today the second busiest bridge in New York City.

Charles River Bridge, Boston. The cable-stayed Charles River Bridge was completed in 2001 with a unique design. It has upside down Y-shaped towers. It is 1,457 feet (444 m) long.

Quebec Railway Bridge, Quebec. After two disasters here, the Quebec Railway Bridge over the St. Lawrence river was completed in 1917. With a length of 1,800 feet (549 m), this cantilever bridge was for some time the world's longest span.

Golden Gate Bridge, San Francisco. Completed in 1937, the Golden Gate stretches 8,981 feet (2,737 m) across San Francisco Bay. It connects San Francisco and Sausalito. Its longest span is 4,200 feet (1,280 m). Engineer Joseph Strauss designed this suspension bridge to stand up to fog, tides, winds, and earthquakes.

Luling Bridge, New Orleans. With its span of 2,746 feet (837 m) across the Mississippi River, the Luling is one of the longest cable-stayed bridges in the United States.

Sunshine Skyway, St. Petersburg, FL. The cable-stayed Skyway's longest span is 1,200 feet (366 m). But the entire bridge reaches 29,040 feet (8,851 m) across Tampa Bay. Completed in 1987, the bridge has won many awards for beauty and design.

Chesapeake Bay Bridge-Tunnel, VA. This beam bridge loops over and under the open waters of Chesapeake Bay in a chain of tunnels, bridges, and artificial islands. It links southeast Virginia to the Delmarva Peninsula. The longest span is just 100 feet (30 m), but the bridges together are about 15 miles (24 km) long.

Port Mann Bridge, Vancouver, British Columbia. The Port Mann Bridge is one of North America's most impressive steel arch bridges. Its main span is 1,200 feet (366 m). Crossing the Fraser River, it was completed in 1964.

Verrazano-Narrows Bridge, New York City. Linking Staten Island and Brooklyn, the Verrazano-Narrows Bridge is one of several important bridges in New York City. This suspension bridge, stretching 4,260 feet (1,298 m) was completed in 1964.

Confederation Bridge, Prince Edward Island and New Brunswick. The Confederation Bridge crossing Northumberland Strait is the world's longest bridge over ice-covered waters. This beam bridge, completed in 1996, is 8 miles (13 km) long.

Lions Gate Bridge, Vancouver, British Columbia. The unique Lions Gate Bridge was completed in 1939. It's a 2,778-foot (847-m) suspension bridge that uses cables made of wire ropes instead of parallel wires.

GLOSSARY

abutment (eh BUT ment) — the structures at the ends of bridges that support a bridge against the ground

anchorage (ANG ker ij) — reinforced concrete structures in which cables are fixed in place

architect (ARH ke tekt) — a person who designs structures

architecture (AHR keh tek cher) — the art or science of building

bent (BENT) — a bridge support, like a pier, but with two pillars under its cap

cable-stayed (KAY bel STAYD) — a type of bridge in which the bridge deck is supported by cables attached directly to the tower

cantilever (KAN te lev er) — a type of bridge in which a section of the span projects beyond its point of support, like a diving board

client (KLY ent) — one who hires someone to do a job

cofferdam (KAWF er dam) — a structure to keep water out of an area that is underwater

compression (kum PRESH en) — a force that reduces or shortens something by pressure

concrete (KAHN kreet) — a building material made by mixing stone or sand with cement and water

contractor (KAHN trak ter) — a person or company that is hired to construct a bridge or other structure

deck (DEK) — the bridge beams or girders on which cars or people can travel; the roadway of a bridge

dissipate (DIS eh payt) — to spread out to decrease the effect of force

engineer (en jeh NEER) — one who uses science and math to design various structures

form traveler (FORM TRAV el er) — a moving form; the mold into which liquid concrete is poured

geologist (je AHL eh jist) — a scientist who studies the Earth

meteorologist (mee tee er AHL eh jist) — a scientist who studies climates and the weather

parallel (PEAR a lel) — that which follows alongside a path or course always at the same distance apart, like rails of a train track

pier (PEER) — a vertical support, such as a column or pillar, for the middle spans of a bridge, or the base of the tower for a bridge

rebar (REE bar) — a framework of steel bars that is filled with concrete

span (SPAN) — to cross over something; or a section of a bridge that crosses over the water

suspension (suh SPEN shun) — the state of hanging in such a way as to be free on most or all sides

tension (TEN shen) — a force that lengthens something

tower (TOW er) — the tall vertical structure onto which cables are attached (cable-stayed) or braced (suspension) on some bridges

truss (TRUS) — short beams or girders that, through a triangle framework, give strength to bridge beams

INDEX

Further Reading:

Doherty, Mary and Glassman, Bruce. *The Golden Gate Bridge.*
  Blackbirch, 1995

Johmann, Carol and Rieth, Elizabeth. *Bridges!* Williamson, 1999

Macaulay, David. *Building Big.* Houghton Mifflin, 2000

Websites to Visit:

www.pbs.org/wgbh/buildingbig

www.bridgepros.com

www.dot.state.ga.us/homeoffs/bridge-design